NINO GUGUNISHVILI

From My Balcony to Yours

First edition

This book was professionally typeset on Reedsy.
Find out more at reedsy.com

"It was the best of times, it was the worst of times, it was the age of wisdom, it was the age of foolishness, it was the epoch of belief, it was the epoch of incredulity, it was the season of Light, it was the season of Darkness, it was the spring of hope, it was the winter of despair..."

Charles Dickens, A Tale of Two Cities

Contents

I

March 2020

1

A Letter to Coronavirus

Dear Coronavirus,

It's without a single regret that I have to reject your offer of taking me on a journey in which I have absolutely no intention or interest to participate. For your information, I've herewith enclosed several points to highlight why. I sincerely hope you'll find them convincing, and I also hope our tête-à-tête meeting will be timely postponed to an unknown future.

So, here are the issues I'd like to highlight and draw to your immediate attention.

1) I've never eaten falafel! Yes, no matter how strange it may sound, falafel is what I intend to eat first thing when self-isolation and social-distancing are over. No, I don't like alcohol. Just a glass of red wine on Friday evenings, preferably. I also want to eat Mille-Feuille, and the tastiest one I've ever had is very far from where I live, so you get the point. You'd probably wonder why all of my wishes are gastronomical. Still, you should probably know that eating is related to pleasure, and pleasure is related to happiness, and happiness means endorphins!

2) I definitely have to go to the sea. I've downloaded an exercise app, and I'm now regularly doing knee tucks, and planks and there's no doubt

I'll have a perfect body for the summer. It's bikini time! Do you even know what Bikini is? Well, in short, it's a socio-cultural phenomenon.

3) I'm planning to meet up with my friends regularly. Please, also be aware that we're planning to travel excessively. Yes, 'travel' will soon be the new "fifty is the new forty," "orange is the new black" type of trend. I advise you to note that.

4) Soon, I'll own a house; I also plan to have two dogs and a cat. Maybe even a horse, a donkey, and a goat! I'll have to adjust to living outside the city, decorate that house with a garden, and live there whenever I want. Please, keep in mind, there's no room to interfere, and don't you dare ruin that plan.

5) I have to write books. Novels, stories, essays. I don't want to bore you with details. Let's just say I have to write. And, also read, watch TV and films, and simply lay on the couch and be a couch potato and never feel guilty about it, walk in the streets of my beautiful city, and many other cities in the world.

6) I plan to get unapologetically drunk at a wedding with all the singing and dancing.

7) I need to buy a coffee machine and drink gazillions of Nespresso and blissfully smoke cigarettes on my balcony or outside the cafes and restaurants. Oh, and please, do not worry about my consumer passions or my bad habits. They allow me to stress, are none of your business.

8) Lastly, let me remind you that 'La Vita e Bella,' no matter how hard you try to prove otherwise.

Yours sincerely,
Fill in the blanks as appropriate

2

Balcony Blues

9:00 am First thought as I wake up is what if I would never have a chance of going anyplace further than the supermarket across my apartment building. I know it's not original to start a story with a "wake up" scene, but specific rules change under the circumstances, don't they?

9:30 am Checking Facebook. Logging off. Checking Instagram. Logging off. Checking Twitter. Love Twitter.

9:45 am Coffee time! God bless whoever decided that our nine-floor apartment building would have balconies. I feel eternally grateful for the opportunity of having a cup of coffee in the fresh air and only looking around. Not that I see anything unusual or unfamiliar. There are parked cars everywhere—an empty stadium, where two boys are coming to every evening with their dogs. I can even tell you the exact time. Usually, it's around 9 pm. For the rest, it's all peace and calm except stray cats wandering around trash bins. To tell you the truth, the view from my balcony doesn't fuel my imagination. Still, the enormous twenty-three-floor building that I wholeheartedly detested suddenly gives me an unexpected hope. Wait, I hated it for so many reasons! For blocking the beautiful view of the TV Tower and a little old church up on the hill, for transforming our street into the never-ending traffic jam, for being so huge compared to the red brick house next to it, and for invading our privacy! But today, seeing that grey building as I'm standing on the balcony brings hope. Someday very soon, new people will be living there, buying croissants in the French bakery across the street, hurrying to their offices, having late-night home parties. It'll be filled with human voices, stories, dramas, heartbreaks, laughter, life.

10:15 am Changing place. Following the recent recommendation, we have to move around the house, so I'm moving. This time I choose to have a quick cigarette on another balcony overlooking the utterly empty park. No joggers, no babies, no dogs.

11:30 am Checking the news on TV makes me want to run somewhere or better sleep until this global virus threat is over. Since running is not an option, and the perspective of living on Mars is still blurred and uncertain, I decide to have a nap, but my super energized friend calls and interrupts me. I feel guilty. She's a hero; I'm a parasite. She's managed to stock up, prepare dinner, take care of her kids, and even bought a belated present for our mutual friend. At times like these, I feel like an alien with no social skills.

12 pm Coffee again. Turkish coffee time. I wonder if I'll ever have a chance of going to Istanbul? If I do, eating that delicious baklava will be the first on my to-do list.

1:00 pm Starting a workout. Honestly? It's very uncomfortable! My mat is at the pilates studio, and the pilates studio is closed. I'm trying. It's just an eight-minute workout, but right now, it feels endless. I combine it with a dance workout, and I'm moving around my living room, clapping hands and smiling. Smile, the trainer says, is essential. The construction worker from the grey building sees my movements. I suspect he's staring at me and maybe thinks I'm nuts, but I have to control my breath according to the workout, and I don't care.

2 pm My cousin calls and says that everything is happening for a reason. We're entering into a short, somewhat philosophical discussion about human nature and time and past and possible future, and she offers me to bring a pumpkin soup.

3 pm - 4 pm. Checking Facebook. Chatting with friends who seem to be online 24/7. Catching up on everything from global to local, from personal to private. I feel like an alien again. Do aliens have a sense of humor?

6 pm I'm trying to hide in reading, but instead, the last trip to Paris comes to my mind, and panic fills up. I don't even want to go deeper into what I'm thinking. Too many "what if's..."

7 pm - 8 pm. Maybe I should buy wine and more chocolate. Or better, Vodka!

9 pm -11 pm God bless HBO and Netflix!

3

Dance, Dance, Dance!

I didn't want to get out of bed today. I couldn't find the reason why I had to, why I couldn't snuggle in bed for the whole day. What did I have to do that needed jumping out and throwing myself into a routine? I could bring my laptop to my bedroom and connect with the outer world from there. Who'd care? Then I could go to sleep, wake up and sleep some more. Luckily, the more optimistic part of me decided that there are better rejuvenating ways, and I got out of my bedroom for coffee, news, and the social media frenzy. It seemed the world stood in the exact same place as yesterday. The virus outbreak, self-isolation, quarantine, social distancing, and clusters are the words we hear and use most often.

My immediate 'cluster' of friends is okay. Each handling the self-imposed stay at home time differently, ranging from mild panic to existential crises blended with self-irony and humor of all imaginable shades (read dark). All the usual remedies of taking our minds off from the downpour of negative news, like reading or watching TV shows and movies, didn't seem to work this time, at least for me. I need something more substantial, mind-blowing, tiring, and freeing. Something that would make me forget my weight, my double-chin, and my thinning hair. I need to see a happier face in the mirror today. Try dancing! I tell myself, but the lazy part of me starts laughing hysterically.

Dancing? Oh, come on, you're no Beyoncé! It said while I was already slowly moving on a silver-colored chaise longue cover mat, grooving, wabbling. Yes, "Dance like no one is watching," dancing, like I was back into my twenties dancing, that truly felt liberating and easy and fun, and as I tried to keep my breath intact, I remembered my pilates teacher saying: "Keep your head up, pretend you're a beautiful swan!" So next time I might dance that little swan dance from the Swan Lake, remember? Have too much time to practice it anyway.

4

Coffees, Cigarettes, and Farida

I t seems they are everywhere, scattered around the house. Small and big, heavy and light, used and new. Our house smells of coffee and cigarettes. We've been a family of smokers, and in between us four, only my mother quit some twenty years ago, but I can still remember her smoking those slim and long cigarettes I can't recall the brand anymore. Seated in an armchair in our living room, she smoked, puffing out rather than inhaling, wrapped in a cloud of smoke.

As I washed my hands for the third time in a row, I glanced down to the bathroom floor and saw it again. Again, because I've seen it countless times, that massive silver ashtray in the bathroom. No one uses it anymore. You know why? Because the reading in a bathroom habit is now gone. The bathroom is no longer a place to hide from your family members.

He was a heavy smoker, my dad, much to the discomfort of my mother. He never tried to quit. It wasn't just a simple act of smoking a cigarette. It was a pleasurable and elaborate ritual he started his mornings with. One cigarette after breakfast, one before going to work, many in the afternoons, and even more in the evenings. Almost two packs a day. If you see the picture of my dad and then me, the resemblance is striking. Our face features, hands, lips, noses are very much alike. I, too, do smoke, not as much as he did, but I also find it pleasurable—especially the first one in the mornings.

He loved drinking a cup of a Turkish coffee that Farida, a Yezidi woman, helping my mom with the house, made for him. Farida had long brown hair and dark black eyes. For a long time, I considered her to be the best fortune-teller. Every time she came, we had to drink coffee and listen to what she had to say regarding our future, but even more, I liked her telling the story of how she took her little son and traveled to Komi, one of the places in the ex-Soviet Union where prisoners were held. Farida's husband was serving his sentence there. I don't know why I was so fascinated with this particular episode of her life. Probably I admired her bravery of taking risks and going to the dangerous journey in the name of love, despite the many obstacles on her way—a long and tiring train journey and living in some kind of barrack for several months. In the comfort of my own safe world, it looked thrilling and romantic. As I understood it, Farida was the closest to the Gipsy culture I could get, and although she always declined to have Gipsy ancestors, for me, back then, in my ten, twelve years of age, she was a Gipsy. She represented a different world; she was surrounded by a mysterious, rebellious flare, her language, a mixture of Georgian, Russian, and Yazidi. She loved face creams and espadrilles. She tolerated our unwillingness to understand that Yezidis were neither Gipsy nor Kurds; it was Farida who made us appreciate and love others, even if we didn't understand them.

She seemed to have a unique ability to interpret what those tiny ornaments and figures on the bottoms of our coffee cups meant. "You'll have a call in three days, and that call will change your life,' she'd exclaim, inhaling nicotine. "Who?! Who's gonna call?" I'd scream. "Someone with the name starting with L, or M, I don't know, and that's enough! I have to make Beef Stroganoff; your dad will be home any minute now!" She'd say, jumping from a kitchen chair, meaning the coffee drinking session was over, and the magic cooking session was about to start. I think it's with Farida I caught the link of coffee and cigarettes being an inseparable duo. She taught me how to prepare Turkish coffee, but I was a horrible learner. Every time I tried, I failed. I fail even now.

She was a great cook, but none of her prophesies ever came true. As we grew up, married, and had children, she transformed into a nanny and helped every family around us. We smoked our first cigarettes together with her, and she kept it secret. Smoking freely wasn't considered as a part of our liberal upbringing. You couldn't smoke in the company of your parents, god forbid in the company of your teachers or lecturers. It was a habit that no one would encourage you to follow, a divide between the world of ours and theirs of parents and children.

One of the first things my dad told me when sending me to study abroad was, "I really hope you won't start smoking..." Oh, I did. Everyone did. All my girlfriends did. What were you supposed to do in Paris?! Even back in Tbilisi, much of our everyday socializing was always connected to smoking. We smoked everywhere except in the streets since smoking involved a certain level of intimacy, and you'd hardly find a teenage girl or a grown-up woman smoking in the street. We smoked because it was cool; it was a way of communicating and bonding with each other. Best secrets were told while smoking on the balconies and hiding cigarette puffs in our bags. If you had beautiful little attributes like a cigarette case or an unusual lighter, you could suggest yourself the coolest! I accidentally broke my father's silver Dupont lighter the very last time we went to Gagra, Abkhazia. I remember that moment very well. I'm standing in the sand, holding the lighter, lazy to march up the stairs, and give it to him. Instead, I throw it up in the air, hoping he'll, of course, catch it, but I miss, and I see the lighter landing on the sun-warmed rock near me. It's damaged.

The next summer, the war began. I remember my brother bringing his Zippo lighter from New York. Bandanas and Zippos quickly became a trend in Tbilisi of the nineties, together with Sinead O'Connor's and Lisa Stansfield's songs.

Mom keeps that damaged Dupont lighter in the cupboard box somewhere.... I saw Farida at my father's funeral twelve years ago and at my uncle's funeral last year. She has decided to become a baptized Christian. Sometimes she travels to France to visit her son, living there now, and I know she still has so many stories to tell. I'm gonna invite her over for a cup of her signature Turkish coffee.

5

Manicure, Hair and Oh, La, La ...

I think it was my aunt that gave me an electric manicure kit on my birthday many years ago. So many years ago, in fact, that I had no idea how to use it, stored it into a cupboard, and, after not much of thinking, gifted it away. Oh, what an idiot I was! But how was I supposed to know that in less than twenty-five years from there, we would find ourselves living in reality, where a simple manicure and pedicure routine would become hard to obtain luxury? That whether to invite or not to invite manicure specialists to our home would almost equal an act of heroism?

The same goes for hair. Goodbye highlights, "Chatouche," asymmetric bobs, and extensions! And have you stocked up your depilatory creams and waxing essentials? Lucky you, if yes, is the answer.

My very recent fear is that in two more weeks of self-isolation, I'll resemble a Lumberjack. My body will be toned due to excessive exercising; the cellulite will be gone, my legs will get muscular and maybe even longer, but! I'll have a beard! Well, as the saying goes, nobody's perfect!

Clearly, instead of worrying about my lack of cooking skills, I should have watched the youtube brow trimming tutorials more. Instead of regretting not learning riding a bicycle, I should have honed applying manicure to my right hand with my left hand. Instead of learning to play guitar, which I never succeeded in, by the way, I should have mastered mixing the right amount of hair dye. Oh, I just discovered a pair of brand new plastic gloves from an old hair coloring set. Invaluable treasure!

6

Canceled Plans, No Plans, Future Plans...

From the moment we wake up, we're planning the day ahead, we try to keep to the schedule, make our to-do lists, customize them, adjust them, and change them, but we're still planning or re-planning. We hold ourselves busy; we need to know and control what lays ahead. We need to have future plans. The future needs to be foreseeable. We need to know what's in there for us because everything we're doing today is future. But the thing is, for the last month, or the last several weeks, the world seems to have canceled every plan it had. Conferences, meetings, even the Olympic Games are either postponed or canceled.

We're sitting in our homes, glued to our phone and computer screens, holding our breaths and waiting for what's going to happen next. What's the plan? What's the scenario? What's the future? For how long are we going to stay home? When is the self-isolation going to end? We need to know because we think we can control when we know, and when we handle, we can plan, and planning means going back to normal. But what if all this Coronavirus story is about shifting the focus and not being so obsessed with planning and controlling and wanting to know what's next? What if it's all about enjoying what we have right now, at this very moment, and not worrying about the future? Not worrying about what we weren't able to do because of the pandemic, but enjoying what we did nevertheless while our plans were ruined? It can be as simple as walking your dog, reading a book, chatting with your friend or your family member over the phone, or getting rid of the unnecessary things at home?

I guess what we come to understand is that ruined plans are not a catastrophe. That we can't and don't have to control everything around us and worry. That right now, we can be happy just because we're alive. The future can wait.

7

Sunday Thoughts After Reading Nora Ephron

What I miss:
  Dad.
  My dog.
My friend Keti.
Augusts in Gagra, Abkhazia.
Winters in Bakuriani.
Snow.
Long hair.
Jeans shorts.
Calling my friends on a landline.
Homemade apple pies.

What I don't miss:
  Office.
  90ies.
  Low-rise jeans.
  Knitted gloves.
  Blond highlights.
  Red hair.

Pre-internet era.
Chicken bullion.
Hot summers.

8

Monday?

What day is it today? Monday? It took me several seconds to remember. Not that I really care. I'll probably be doing the same on Tuesday, Wednesday, and Thursday, and Friday. I'll be here in my living room glued to my couch on the weekend, next week, and the week after. Days pass in the same rhythm, and guess what? I like it. I don't really understand why people are complaining so much about being home.

I get that it's tough to obey the rules and keep yourself self-isolated, and it's tough not to go out when you can't stand being locked at home for any second more, but what if, in the worst-case scenario, things will get so bad, we gonna miss this self-isolation? What if we'll remember this time as one of the happiest? Because the truth is we don't really know what's going to happen next. The truth is we can only hope for the best. Hope that we'll be visiting each other and spending time together and traveling. Going out in the evenings, attending film premieres and concerts, and having Mojitos, champagne or wine afterward, we'll be going to our offices on Monday, looking forward to weekends. We'll be exhausted, and we'll be motivated, and sometimes bored, and sometimes joyful, and sometimes very sad.

All of it seems surreal now. Life has changed in the blink of an eye. Have we? Will we be different when the Coronavirus outbreak passes? Are we going to change our habits or goals and ambitions when it's over? Or are we going to stay just as we are? What are we going to gain from all this experience? Something? Anything? Are we going to hate Mondays again collectively? I don't know If you, dearest reader, do, please, let me know. In the meantime, all that comes to my mind is: "everything's going to be okay in the end. If it's not okay, it's not the end." And seriously, from now on, I'm gonna love Mondays!

9

A Groundhog Day

O n one of the days in May of 1985, my mother insisted on putting iodine on my knees and elbows before I ran out to play with other kids in the yard, and then I remember it rained. It was several days, maybe a week later, after Chernobyl. I remember my closest friend telling me that her cousin came from Kiyev to Tbilisi, and they had to burn all of her clothes. We knew something terrible happened; we sensed it was a huge change, a catastrophe, but knowing it, didn't affect our daily lives. In the safe cocoon of our childhoods, it seemed its outcomes would not reach us. Several years later, the Soviet Union collapsed, swiping us with a tornado of changes, and maybe out of pure egoism or unconscious fear, we hid Chernobyl in the back of our minds, forgetting and remembering it when convenient.

Yesterday evening, as we sat and watched Homeland's latest episode, my mom and I agreed that historically there were more dramatic things happening than Coronavirus. From armed conflicts and endless wars, from Fukushima, tsunamis, earthquakes, forest fires in Australia to the almost ruined Notre Dame Cathedral last summer.

"Do you have your bucket list ready?" my friend asked when we heard about Fukushima. "Not really," I replied, and we went back to planning the monthly TV grid. We were frightened, of course, but once again, we selfishly thought it wouldn't reach us. We went to a self-defendant, egoistic, survival, half ignorance, half acceptance mode. Fast forward to the winter of 2020... The new Coronavirus epidemic hits, affecting everything and everyone everywhere.

We're washing hands and staying home, socially distanced and self-isolated. We're frightened. We're uncertain. We're lost, we're panicking, we're grieving, we're hoping, we're following news from all over the world, we're optimistic, we're pessimistic, it's here, right at our doors, behind our backs, in front of us, reachable, tangible, dangerous, real, yet controllable. I wonder where are we going to be in a year from now? Back to normal? But what that *normal* is going to be? Are we going to live by the newly imposed rules? Most of all, I wonder what children are thinking about it. How do they see it, and what they feel. Most of all, I want to see them carelessly playing football at the stadium. Right now, Tbilisi is so calm, it feels like a never-ending Sunday.

II

April 2020

10

Fool's Day

Someone fooled us big! Someone did a massive prank. Someone decided we should be locked in. Someone made us stop in our tracks and postpone everything to an undetermined future. Someone wanted us to enjoy this Spring from our homes, and instead of exposing our faces and bodies to the Spring sun, explore the palettes on our walls, count them, recount them, and generally excel in math. I need seventeen steps to get from my living room to the kitchen. I also know what my neighbors from upstairs are doing during different parts of the day. They're listening to music and watching TV 24/7. We have a very different musical taste, but I accept that difference wholeheartedly. They, on the other hand, are incredibly tolerant of my loud-speaking on the phone. I've also found out how most of my friends looked like when they were children, thanks to the photos they're posting on Facebook, and if a year ago I'd be skeptical or ironic about it, today, on April 1, 2020, I find it very sweet, nostalgic and uplifting. And the tremendous amount of life-hacks and recommendations coming from everywhere?

Why did we hide it for so long? If there were so many movies to watch, books to read, museums to visit online, so many courses we could take from cooking to astrophysics? Why didn't we share? I'm not sure about astrophysics, but you get the point. I mean, what were we doing before this lockdown? Let's be honest; we were doing nothing. The world seems to be busier today. Twenty-four hours are not enough for all we want to do and all we have to. Disinfecting products, washing hands, washing clothes, following the rules of going out for a short trip to a supermarket and getting back, inventing new routes for dog walks, inventing new recipes for home cooking, exploring the patience limits our family members possess. All of that takes a lot of time and energy, and skills. Speaking of new skills, my friend recently suggested we try an online group Tango class or Cha -Cha. One two three, one two three, one two three....

11

Here Comes the Sun...

Here comes the sun, and it's Friday, and it's April, and it's gorgeous weather outside. This time last year, I was in Paris. I scrolled through the photos from that trip last year, and it made me sad. In fact, it made me think that we're ungrateful for what we already have, that we tend to take so many things for granted, easy to achieve, and stable.

If someone told me last year that we'd all be locked in our houses, that the world would be fighting Coronavirus and that we would hear the devastating news from everywhere daily, I would never have believed it. Nor could I imagine that the sense of time passing unexplainably slow would be so vivid, bringing back the memories of summers in my childhood, when a three-month school break felt like an eternity and September seemed to be so, so far. I'm having the same "slow-motion" deja vu these days, while at the same time being home brings a sense of safety and comfort. I don't want to be anywhere but home now; it's the coziest, the warmest place to be, but I've always wanted to leave it, I've always wanted to live someplace else, return and travel again. I've always thought I had no particular attachment to where I lived. As strange and naïve as it may sound, I've just recently understood that coming home is the most emotional, vital part, that the possibility of always returning home is what makes travel enjoyable. Maybe that's why we travel after all?

My latest "travel destinations" are my apartment balconies and the sunrises you can watch from there are beautiful. How come I've never seen them before?

12

If

If I were to be a character, I would choose to be a heroine from a Chick-lit book right now. I'd have my fair share of heartbreaks and hurdles, but eventually, I would get to the point where I would want to be. I would be funny and smart and ironic and humble, and I would be sassy, yes, why not? In other words, I would be a strong female character as opposed to the neurotic, hesitant, frightened human being I am right now. I would be adventurous. I would get myself into a mind-blowing romance! I would meet the love of my life accidentally! I would tackle the different life situations with zest and grit and make my dreams and aspirations come true. I wouldn't wait for tomorrow's ever. I would seize the moment and try to be happy.

I've never been a Sci-Fi or Fantasy fan, neither in movies nor in literature. Ironically right now, we're living in a reality where everything we've seen or read in that genre seems to be coming true. We became characters of the sci-fi thriller and can only hope that there will be a happy ending. There is no other way this thriller the world is currently watching and living in to end. The happy end is the only possible option. The comfortable, cheesy, and most tear-jerking happy ending one could think of, only this time off-screen, in real life. If anyone ever underestimated the power of Chick Lit or Romance, now I guess it is the exact time to rethink it. We need now life-affirming love stories and humor, and more Bridget Jones's or Carrie Bradshaw's!

13

The Suitcase Blues

I spotted my big black suitcase with a red ribbon tied on its handle this morning, and suddenly it felt so out of place in that half-storage, half- study room jammed with old cupboard boxes, notebooks, books, and toys still on the shelves. The suitcase with which I've traveled around to everywhere from Istanbul to Rome stood there as a sad dinosaur, a relic from the past, as a lonely artifact transforming into the symbol of unexpected, uncontrollable change. I've never been good at packing, and I never liked airports, and yet, travel, no matter how far I went, always brought me to the most pleasurable, fun, unforgettable moments I've ever experienced in my life, whether with friends, family, or on my own, solo. And as selfish as it is now, what I'm thinking is how we will adjust to the fact that we will not be able to travel at least for several months if not for more? When are we going to buy plane tickets and land in Paris or Barcelona, or Rome again? When are we going to explore the places we've never been to? Soon? Not so soon? Never? And what's with all the advice on where exactly to go, what to taste and see, and where to stay? Imagine how many lists we've done, the articles we've saved, the notes we've made of our "must do's" now seem useless. ''What about comfy shoes for endless strolls in the cities and checking our mobile apps on how many steps we made? What about sightseeing blanded with gourmet feasts and new discoveries? What about the favorite coffee spots and bookstores and gift shops? What about going to crowded touristy places and hidden gems and secret passages of the cities? What about mountain resorts? What about the Bateaux Mouches and trains and trams and the hop -on the hop-off bus tours? Is all of it in the past, or will they wait for us with our selfie-sticks ready, gleefully looking into the camera in front of Louvre, or MET, or Boboli gardens, sometimes, next year maybe?

The movie title "Last Summer in Marienbad" comes to my mind. I've never been to Marienbad, by the way.

14

Eat, Sleep, Read, Watch, Repeat!

Morning and afternoon coffees -done.

Zoomba Workout - done.

Indian Dance Workout -done.

Facebook, Instagram, Twitter -Checked.

I spoke with my cousin. She made a Zebra, a house pie with chocolate. Brought the homemade Zebra to us. Had some sort of a posh mask on—the anti-virus one.

Lunch - done.

Local news, international news watched.

Facebook, Instagram, Twitter -Checked.

Facebook, Instagram, Twitter -Checked.

My friend bought a ping-pong table.

Switched to water with lemon not to be over-caffeinated.

Facebook, Instagram, Twitter -Checked

"Here are five simple recipes to make while you're staying home," my Facebook feed reads. "Here are the five best movies to watch while you're self-isolating."

"Here are five short books to read while you're self-distancing, here are five long books for you while at home, here are the best apps for you to learn a new language while the entire world is in lockdown... here are the 10 plants you can quickly grow on your balcony... here are the 100 TV shows to watch from here to eternity! And on this advice goes and seriously, I'm entirely dumbstruck and lost in the sea of all this information. I can't digest it.

Stray dogs are wandering through the streets.

Cats are more likely to get infected with Coronavirus than dogs.

No, dogs don't get Coronavirus.

Tiger at the Bronx's zoo tested positive for Coronavirus.

There will be a vaccine soon.

The vaccine won't be ready at least for a year from now.

Washing hands gives a sense of safety, the doctor on TV said.

I'm washing my hands. Smoking. Washing hands. Smoking. Washing hands.

The snow was in the forecast yesterday.

There's no snow today.

My friend brought me Lasagna and sweets. She's my cluster. I'm her cluster. Another friend wrote a sweet letter to us in our Facebook group, saying she loves us all, despite our differences. We assured her we loved her back, to the moon, to the stars, to the Mars and Jupiter and back. She has a fluffy white hamster. Two of them locked in.

I'm afraid of hamsters.

I'm afraid of starving street dogs.

I'm afraid of becoming three sizes bigger while I'm at home.

I want to shave my head. My friends look at me very suspiciously when I say it loud.

I'm afraid. I'm okay.

Am I?

15

Linked to the World with USB

My phone's USB cable silently died yesterday afternoon. The phone showed it had only 30% of battery remaining. One round of game away, one phone call away, and then the battery meter would turn into that dangerous red color and turn off, oh the horror, leaving me discharged from the outside world. The tiny white USB cable laid on the table with no chance of being reanimated despite my numerous efforts. A lifespan too short. "What shall we do?" My mother asked, poorly hiding panic in her tone. Really, what could we do without our phones? Without the evening ritual of checking with family? Without logging into social media? Messaging? Watching Youtube? Without knowing what our friends made for dinner? How could we survive without all of these tidbits due to the unexpected damage of that silly USB cable?

You'd say all of the abovementioned can be done on a computer too, or Ipad. Yes. But the phone is different. Your phone is you. All essential things, everything that matters to you personally, is squeezed in there, from notes to photos, and passwords, and memories. We are spoiled with the comfort of being immediately reached, satisfying the surge of accessing anything instantly. Patience is long gone with the landlines.

Who's calling on landlines these days? Sometimes I can't even remember my own number.

Those several hours before I got the new USB cable seemed endless. I feared something significant was happening out there, and I would be completely cut out of it, like Robinson Crusoe, which I have to admit was never my favorite character. When the new USB finally arrived, I plugged in my phone and discovered my friend had a great day. She went to the supermarket and bought whiskey, gin, and wine!

16

1000 Steps

My Converse sneakers on my bedroom floor, my Clinique foundation in a tiny bag, next to the lipstick, tweezers, and bronzing powder. Two perfume bottles and an eyeshadow set I haven't used in ages. Funny, I might not use any of these at least for another month or more. Next in the list of useless items is SPF -30 sun protector cream. Right now, I'm overprotected from sun rays! I'm in desperate need of sunlight and vitamin D, and I'm running to the balcony on any occasion. From my frequent errands, I found out that my neighbor in the next apartment building got mail.

I saw a mail courier on a blue bike. Also, two new Shih Tzu dogs I've never seen before, but enough of dogs, back to decluttering. There are four pairs of black pants in my wardrobe. I don't need any of them right now. Two white shirts? I don't even work at the office. My office is my living room, sometimes my kitchen, or my study. Forgot about the shimmering body lotion I found on the shelve next to the hairdryer. Completely useless. It's not summer yet; no need to shimmer. Who's gonna see my shimmering shoulders? No one. Next, the hair curlers I found hidden under the jewelry box. They're from the other era, from the time I wore round glasses with a slight violet glow, circa fifteen years ago.

I'm probably addicted to scarves and shawls or have developed a fetish towards them; there's no other way to understand why I have so many. In different colors, lengths, patterns, and fabric. Pashminas, short ones, red ones, green ones, grey ones, and black ones, of course. Don't need them either, unless it becomes windy on my balcony. I like the world patio more, although my balcony is not a patio at all, just in case you wonder. One scarf is missing. My long, brown wool scarf, which I gifted away because it was too long and too warm, and whenever I wore it, my friend worried I'd either step on it accidentally or suffocate. You have to sacrifice some things for friendships....

Lastly, there are bags. What did I think when I bought them? Where was I planning to go? These giant, heavy bags with big compartments for files, cosmetic purses, notebooks, and pens... It seems I'll never use them again. They seem to belong to another person, not me, to someone I don't recognize anymore. By the time I finish inspecting my useless belongings, the steps tracker on my phone shows I made 1000 steps, 1000 steps for a weird journey in time. I need to change my socks now, of which I have plenty. Socks are my best friends!

17

Sixty Capsules of Happiness

"Change the water six times," the instruction to my new family member, a dark black, silvery coffee machine said. I followed the instructions thoroughly. The Brazilian roast capsule disappeared into the black abyss, but there was no Voila! Instead, the hot water poured down into the china teacup, duly taken from the cupboard for this exceptional occasion.

Delicately I took out the capsule and threw it into the trash bin. I tried one more time in vain. The Brazilian roast capsule was soon followed by Guatemalan, El Salvador, and Vanilla to the trash. The coffee machine refused to adapt to the new surroundings of my kitchen and rebelled.

"You're probably not doing something right," Mom said and recommended to read the printed instructions again. I did. She did. Then I Facetimed Maya, my friend, who's been an experienced coffee machine owner for ages. Maya's suggestions shed some light on the mystery of coffee making. Finally, after two more unsuccessful attempts, there it was, Brazilian coffee aroma filling in, its taste robust, sharp, nuanced, delicious! The love at first sip, an instant click, an intimate connection, the thrill, and the anticipation of the new story to be told. The happiness of being alive.

18

A Woman at the Seashore

A red tablecloth, my phone, a pen, a notepad, a candle, a clock, matches. Two TV remotes. Pillows on the sofa. A TV that is mostly switched off. The room is dimly lit. Am I writing a new story? No, I'm just describing what I see in the proximity of one meter. Objects that surround me, the ones I see and interact with every day. There's a painting on the wall from my cousin - a woman sitting on the seashore watching the ship in the distance. She's thinking about something. Maybe she's waiting for someone, or she just had a painful split? Maybe she's about to do something she'd later regret? The ship is too far on the horizon, unreachable. Perhaps it's even a mirage? If she can see an illusion, why can't I see seagulls instead of pigeons and a seaside flower boulevard instead of the empty rainy street outside my window? Why can't my hair be wet from swimming and my skin tasting salty? And why can't I have an afternoon Mimosa cocktail in a nearby café? I don't want to write the word *because.* There are too many reasons why right now, it's all impossible.

But today, I'll pretend I'm that unknown woman sitting by the seashore and dreaming and planning and maybe eating a half-melted chocolate ice –cream afterward.

19

How to Survive Self-Isolation Like a Pro

Hide the scales. Don't hop on them every morning, nurturing a false hope that zillions of workouts will help you become the next top model on the cover of the glossy magazine. Worry about your hair—neither its length nor the color.

Keep in mind that those black velvet pants you're wearing every single day are the new #stayathome chic!

Are you rewatching TV shows you've already seen one hundred times? Keep watching. It would be best if you had all the familiar faces on TV. Most likely, your oxygen-deprived brain won't recognize anyone new. The trick is, you need to say their lines before they start talking. If it seems they're in a lengthy dialogue with you, they probably are. No worries.

Do you feel guilty for not reading anything new from your virtual or physical bookshelves, getting back to the beloved books instead? Don't! Stick to that. That's why they're called 'classics.'

Don't feel ready to follow the trend of honing your cooking skills while at home? Never mind! Try replacing cooking with vacuum cleaning and pretend you're exercising. You might end up in the funniest videos of the decade on Youtube, but your future grandchildren will be proud.

Drink coffee. Everywhere. Change places. Pretend you're traveling. When there's no more coffee left, change to tea or vice versa.

Look out of the window. Do you see the park? Do you see a lonely man walking with a dog in the pouring rain? Now feel it. Feel the joy of not owning a dog, bringing it home, clearing its paws and fur at least three times a day. Congratulations! You're a lucky human. Now inhale and then exhale.

Sleep. Sleep all day. On a couch. In bed. On another couch. Don't be afraid of missing something or someone important while sleeping. The Prince is self-isolated too anyway.

III

May 2020

20

Back to the Future

I don't want to bake bread, for I don't have a single idea how to do it despite the easy recipes shared by my friends who found the process of food making therapeutic and inspiring.

I don't want to exercise at home, learn a new language, or go for a walk. I don't want to buy flowers and see them in vases in my living room. I don't want to shuffle through my wardrobe or table, throwing away the old clothes, old letters, or notebooks. I don't want to throw away unnecessary things. I don't want to find ways of feeling and being comfortable at home. I don't want to be continuously reminded that we will change, the world will change, and we'll have to adapt to the new rules of our existence, with masks and gloves and hand-sanitizers becoming a norm. My mind refuses to acknowledge that strange "newness." Today I want to be as old-fashioned, out-moded, out-dated as one can be.

I want to go back to the Friday-outs and weekend trips and longer voyages; I want to go back to the days when our relatives came for the unexpected lengthy visits, oh, the horror! I want to go back to the time when there were no places in the local restaurants even with reservations, and you'd have to nervously wait outside to be seated. I want that forgotten sense of skipping going out with friends on a weekend evening. I want them to call me lazy, boring, and anti-social... I want to plan something real and tangible and physical ahead. I want this pandemic to have a deadline, a finish line, an end. I want to hear my pilates instructor screaming my name in the class because my body refuses to obey the exercise's rhythm and does something entirely different from any known pilates routine. I want to see movies in theatres, eat popcorn, and then discuss what we saw in a café instead of my kitchen.

I want to go back to the real, not virtual, predictable future ahead: scary, thrilling, hopeful, bewildering.... You can add more adjectives of your own.

21

Grey Cardigan

My grey cardigan has a hole. It's old, I can never wear it outdoors again, but it's okay at home. It's too comfy to throw it out. I know when precisely that tiny hole appeared. I was walking Figu, my dog, and accidentally bumped into an iron stick on the sidewalk. I ignored it and walked on, hurried to the park. Strange, why I remember it now. I can barely remember events from last week or even yesterday. Still, I vividly remember that morning walk from several years ago, a mundane, insignificant thing, a cardigan with a hole is nothing to report about, except for my clumsiness. Is it? Or is it just another justification that I'm continually going back to the past these days, predictable, structured, planned? I do remember when I bought it, though. A few Januaries ago, in New York, we decided to dive into an unnecessary shopping frenzy on one of the days. Instead of buying several things at once, we invented a ritual spread over a week, carefully choosing gloves and warm hats and leggings and leather pants and, of course, cardigans to warm us up that freezing winter.

With no further psychological diggings involved, I know I'll be forever attached to specific memories that resurface now, not in full episodes, just glimpses in flashbacks. Small things that we used to do before the global virus pandemic started seemed so easily achievable; we were sure we'd travel again and return to our loved places. No matter what we planned, we knew we'd have a second try, one more chance, and many more opportunities even if we failed. In short, we were looking forward to the future, which we thought would bring something better to us, a certainty that the future will inevitably be better than the past. I want to be optimistic. I'm trying to, and mostly I'm still sticking to the belief that whatever is ahead will be more thrilling and enjoyable in comparison to the past. Yet, sometimes that optimistic vibe is entirely swallowed by a menacingly growing hole of my old cardigan, setting the former and the new apart, drawing a thick line between the before and the after. Still, I'm not throwing the cardigan away yet.

22

Not a Private Space. Enter!

L et's face it; let's be honest! We've never witnessed such a massive outpour of love before social media existed. We never knew we could express our feelings with such zest before opening our social media accounts with cover images and profile pictures, pictures of ourselves surrounded by our loved ones, our children and family, our friends, and our pets. We had no idea we could be sharing our everyday moments and receiving so much love in return.

We couldn't imagine that so many people cared about what we ate, what we wore, what we bought, how we spent our weekends, or where we went for holidays. All the sympathy, empathy, gratitude, and devotion suddenly merged into one space called social media, enwrapping us all into an endless declaration of how much and how strong we all love each other! Isn't it an ideal place to be? Where else can you find heartwarming toddler and puppy videos? Inspirational Quotes? Find your friend you haven't met since school and would probably never recognize until seeing her in that purple dress at a gala dinner? She surely did something to her chin and eyes, and probably nose as well, but that's none of your business. Following the unwritten rule of social media etiquette, you post a heart sticker under her photo.

Ideally, three hearts, to underline how much you admire her beauty. You're kind. You're not jealous. The same goes for your other friend's fiftieth post featuring four of her children and their dog and her handsome husband on a picnic. You tap the button, and there they are, tiny love signs gleaming! You show your love to your friend, adding "Love you all" and tag her so that you know she sees your comment duly and replies. She sends you one heart in return and tags you back. That's what friends are for! Not that you doubt your long-lasting friendships but still. Here, in this universe of "I love you's," showing your bond matters the most. Love makes this virtual world turn around, and as in every society, here too, we want to be integrated, appreciated, and acknowledged as well-mannered members with super-competent voice, exciting and fulfilled lives, and an excellent taste in everything from food to fashion, to latest hairstyles to best self-care routines. We want to be in the know of the latest trends, and gossips, and all the tiny details of other people's lives.

Because we're all friends here, you know, and friends need to see the news, comment on the story, and share their opinion, advice, their own experience of how to stay on good terms with your ex, what to name your dog, what bras size to wear and where to buy it on sale. Where to go on a date and what places to avoid. How to lose 10 pounds in 10 days, find a dream job in just a week, when exactly to get married, and whether to stay or not to stay friends with your ex-mother -in law.

Here, in this virtual universe of picture-perfect, toned bodies, radiant smiles, and year-round tans, beautiful interiors, gardens, smart and adorable pets, morning breakfasts, and cups of coffees, in the world of gloss and glamour, we're eagerly sharing! Everyone gets their fair share of shares! And don't you ever forget to say *I love you!* That's the code to this world and your path to the crème de la crème of this virtual society. Also, don't forget to master the check-ins. Check-ins are essential to prove you're a valued member of this world. You're locked in due to the pandemic? Still, you can tirelessly show your friends how perfectly you're coping with staying at home! You're fearless; you know how to deal with it! You're an expert! Show it! Let the world see how brilliant you are at everything you do! That's an unwritten rule that you have to scrupulously follow unless you want to be left out from this world inhabited by love, where everyone is welcome.

Of course, you need to see and hear that everyone raves about you and appreciates what a gem of a human you are, with your intellect, sense of humor, in-depth understanding, and knowledge of world politics, history, music, fashion, film, and literature. Even if everyone knows it already, you have to nail it down again and again. You are one of a kind! You are talented; you are smart; you are simply brilliant at navigating this life effortlessly! You care. There's no room for self-doubt! Smile bright, sing, dance, drink wine or cocktails, and always, always, share! That's the only way to receive all the love back. The virtual world is created to radiate happiness. If you're unhappy or lost and unsure, I'm sorry; that's not the right place for you. No one needs to know your worries here. If you want to be a part of this vanity party, play by the rules. Play, and remember to say *I love you* as many times as possible. That's your secret to virtual world domination and endless, eternal happiness!

23

Hide and Zoom!

"Let's Zoom in the evening!" – My friends suggested two days ago. I didn't want to. I was lazy. "Are you ready to Zoom?" They asked again yesterday. I tried to watch " The Good Fight" episode, so I declined. I'm gonna be honest. I'm starting to hate our Zoom meetings—the artificialness of pretending to be okay, joyous, and optimistic.

" Look, I've got my hair colored!" One of us says, oh, what an accomplishment! "I did my pedicure on my own at home!" Another announces, and we congratulate her! "My housekeeper is coming back on Monday!" the third one shares her own upcoming delight, and we all nod smiling from ear to ear, cheering up, mounting our glasses filled with wine, champagne, or Cognac. We're eagerly sharing tidbits of our lives with each other, talking altogether, laughing, and drinking. In our self-distanced living, a zoom meeting is an event not to be missed, and yet I do not like it; I'm starting to hate it almost physically more and more. "Now it's your turn. What you've been up to?" That's the one question I dread. "Sleeping mostly," I reply, although it's not entirely true. I've been reading extensively, and there are days when I'm writing, but I don't want to talk about it while Zooming. It seems irrelevant.

When I lie that I'm sleeping, I'm trying to revert the question to anyone else who's life seems more interesting than mine. I pretend I'm happy that my friend's housekeeper will knock at her door on Monday, returning her to normal, or that another friend is taking her cat to the vet finally because its nails need to be trimmed much like the owner's. Honestly? I want to scream into the screen instead of chatting and nodding and listening. I want to scream that I don't fucking give a damn about my own colored hair, or my friend's unnamed hamster needing a bath, or the productive and smart shopping one of us did. I don't want to see the still unopened rows of bottles on the wine stand. I don't want to pretend we're okay, that we're coping, and we're trying to have fun in the lockdown, and oh, we've learned to appreciate simple things in life and how to slow down, and here we are, rejoicing over how effortlessly we're floundering along. Listen, we're in the age range of 45-48; we're no exuberant teenagers anymore. Our twenties are long gone. How can we be only profoundly concerned with nail trimming, hair coloring, and facials? There must be more existential dilemmas to be solved, in-depth revelations of what worries us, what makes us wake up at six o'clock in the morning, what we fear, but our online meetings scratch the surface just a tiny bit. It seems we're more distanced, paying attention, and fulfilling our apparent needs, shielding away from reality. Hiding.

I need to know why my friend doesn't want to return to her work. I want to see how another friend will solve the prospect of losing her job. I want to yell that I'm afraid all "tomorrow is gonna be another day" might not be relevant anymore. I want to proclaim loud and clear that pseudo –optimism and glaring to the bright future, which is yet to come, can be too time – consuming and tiring sometimes.

I want to know what is really happening. I want to confess that I feel like a mess. I need to know the dark side. The darker and the scarier, the better. Any volunteers? Oh, and by the way, yesterday I bought two tables. Please don't ask me why.

24

The Door's Open

"The door is open ...." No more hiding at home is needed. The public transport resumes working, and at the beginning of June, open space cafes and restaurants will open their doors to the visitors.

We've been waiting for this to happen from the very first day of the lockdown. It's what we've been anticipating, right? Making plans on what we'll do when finally out of our homes. We've been waiting for the pandemic, the lockdown, the social isolation, and self-distancing to end. We were waiting for a full stop, no commas or unfinished sentences, and the faster, the better.

"The door is open; you can go, but remember..." Yes, thanks, it's not over yet. Not over at all. And excuse me, go where? The next sentence that comes to my mind is no, thank you. I'm not ready. I have to adjust to the new rules of social outings if there will be any. Masks or no masks? Two-meter distance or a meter and a half? No hugging and kissing? Gloves or no gloves? Sanitizers?! Too many things to consider! How are we going to meet each other? A group of two? A group of five?

Suddenly I realize that honestly, I don't want to follow these rules and recommendations. At home, it's all too simple and predictable; you can't get infected from merely going from room to room, you don't need a face mask in front of a TV or while glued to your couch, and you can get at least a tiny dose of a vitamin D on your balcony. My friend said she's getting too stressed every time she leaves her house. So am I. I will be. I'll fret for sure. It's like getting out of bed with a vestibular disorder, unable to locate yourself in the space, and feel the distance. Too far? Too close? Where is the danger?

"The thing is, we have no idea what's going to happen tomorrow," my mom said yesterday. We never knew. Never better than now. The trick is, no one can tell us a precise time when all this is going to end. No one knows the exact hour, date, or time. You can't set up the clock. For an unidentified time, we'll be living without knowing.

I have to go to the dentist. Thanks, after you.

IV

June 2020

25

Sometimes...

Sometimes, not often, but sometimes I can't get rid of the feeling that I'm living someone else's life. I can almost physically sense that I'm living in someone else's body, in an unknown city, in an unfamiliar country. I don't like the woman I see in the mirror, that middle-aged lady with glasses twinkling at me. What if I was married and had children? What if I had chosen a different career and profession, and what if I've been a doctor? What if I lived in another country? What if I did everything or at least many things differently? I know, I understand that all these questions I'm asking now lead to nowhere. They don't have answers. What's gone is gone. Chances not taken for various reasons need to be forgotten. There's no one to be blamed except me. Why, on this longest day of summer, I'm now regretting many things that could have been done? It could have been. But it's too late, too far, somewhere in another life, and yet I'm overwhelmed with regret that nothing can be changed or undone.

I'm picturing the seashore. Are we going to go to the sea this summer? I'm afraid. Coronavirus and pandemic are still here. When is it going to end? No one knows. It's hard to survive this summer without the sea. Without the salty water drops on your sun-soaked skin, and curly hair and sunsets and coffee on the hotel balcony and eating grilled fish and tomatoes and milky Georgian cheese... I'd love to have a tiny hut on the beach, in that another life, maybe?!

26

Fear

I 've been used to living with fear for as long as I can remember myself....

Fear of falling and hurting my knees, fear of breaking my glasses, fear of falling down the skateboard, bicycle or the skies, fear of dentists, fear of getting lost, fear of rats and bats and snakes, fear of drowning in the sea.... Fear of getting ill after overeating ice cream, fear of getting burned after spending too much time in the sun, fear of the dark, and many, many more. An overprotected child, a girl, seemed everyone wanted to warn about the outside world's dangers. I don't know why I absorbed these fears so eagerly, why I never protested, why it never crossed my mind that I won't get ill from merely running in the rain or get infected with a virus from eating at the school cafeteria. Having lunch in the school cafeteria or going to the school toilet was out of the question, but of course, we all went to both places and survived. Naturally, we all did something that was a no, no, no, from skipping classes and going to the cinema instead, drinking a bottle of champagne and then adding some vodka mixed with confiture on long summer holidays.

We're now grown-ups. We're smart, responsible, independent women, at least I want to think we are, and most of our childhood fears are long gone. Well, it turns out not entirely; instead of vanishing, they're now transformed, changing their places with other, more profound, primal ones. The fear of losing someone we love, the fear of getting terminally ill, the fear of getting this awful virus, and, most of all, the fear of being unable to live, without bearing in mind that you have to be always on a watch-out, keeping the distance, washing hands, using sanitizer, wearing masks and sometimes gloves....

COVID – is like that noisy, unwanted neighbor you have to share your apartment with, but why do we have so much trouble acknowledging its existence? Why do we need its proof over and over again? Why are we playing the "I'm not as crazy as you" game? Why do we think it'll pass? When?! I believe we are so used to have definite answers on everything; it's the fear of the unknown that drives us crazy. We're so used to holding someone responsible, demanding precise answers, the not knowing makes us vulnerable, and not being in charge of our own lives drives us nuts!

We've always been told that everything will be okay, if not today, then tomorrow, or the day after tomorrow, and suddenly it occurs that this tomorrow may happen in the very, very distant future. What shall we do until then? Dance? Cook? Write? Sing? Paint? Marry? Divorce? Get a cat? Are we staying online or getting offline? Are we traveling from home or not going anywhere until we don't get on the plane? Are we having a cup of coffee at home or in the café? Are we making bucket lists or just plans for the nearest weekend? Are we dead, or are we alive?! Do we exist, or do we live overcoming the fear, even when forgetting to wear a face mask sometime?

27

No Story and Petunias

I don't have a story to tell. My universe is minimized to my living room's size and couch—the one we bought several days ago. If I could post a "no story to tell" sticker, I'd do it. I don't want anyone to know anything new about me, and I'm not very interested in who's doing what among my circle of friends or beneath it.

I don't have a story to tell.... But I do have one that I don't want to tell you. It's about boredom and anxiety and loneliness, and regret. It's about a strange summer. It's about tranquility and calmness, it's about waiting for something beautiful to happen, and maybe it's about a need for change.

I see our pink Petunias on our balcony, energetic and full of life from where I'm seated. Alive! Enjoying the sun and the summer, the long days, the warmth, the rain that poured on them all-day yesterday... They seem to have no worries, no self-pity; they expect the best; I, the human, will take care of them. They don't care what day it is, what year, they don't care about the past or the future, they don't feel nostalgic or sentimental, exist, happy to be alive and present, and don't worry about the failures, old and future ones.

I might post their picture on Instagram.... in the stories....

V

July 2020

28

Magic Forest

Have you ever been to the magic forest, where time stops, and your childhood comes back to you with a tornado speed? Where dark green pine trees stand so tall, they almost cut the sky with their tops? Where it's so calm, you can hear every bird, every frog, every squirrel? When was the last time you went to the place where you've been playing hide and seek or cycling the bicycle? Where has nothing much changed except you?

Returning, remembering, reminiscing, going back, inhaling the smells, walking, and seeing the ones that are no longer alive.

"You were princesses staying at the castles, right?" my friend's twenty-year daughter asked us ironically as her mother told her the story of staying at Russian Emperor Romanov's palace as a young girl, and we agreed, that yes, maybe we were. How much of real us, these children know? Do they know what we loved, what we talked and laughed and worried about, what were our dreams, or our fears, and what we wanted our lives to be? How much of it did we achieve? How many of our childhood dreams did come true? I wonder if these girls are interested in their parents' lives? If they want to know what their lives consisted of before getting married? Before they were 40, and now 46?

Are their joys the same as ours? Do we enjoy the same things, or are they from another planet, baring as many differences as we had with our parents? Do they want to be and act differently? Independently? Will they feel sentimental remembering their childhood and teenage years, as we do? Will they be afraid of the ghosts from their pasts? Will they defend their life choices? What will their regrets be? What will make them happy? What will their most cherished memories be? Will they return to the mysterious forests of their childhood?

VI

August 2020

29

Everyone Says I Love You

For a good half part of my conscious life, I haven't heard the phrase "I love you!" too often. I haven't heard it much either in my childhood, in my teenage years, or through my adult life. Not because I lacked it, no, on the contrary, I was spoiled rotten and showered with love, care, attention, and protection from everyone, especially from my family. Still, I can't recall my parents, my married friends, or couples around me saying "I love you" to each other often, publicly and openly. I guess love was considered something so obvious; there was no need to express it verbally. Maybe by saying, "I love you," we were afraid that from one of the most complex, intangible, intimate feelings, love would transform into something simple and easily accessible, that it would lose its magic? Maybe we were taught to keep its physical, sexual, and sensual aspects for ourselves, in secret, not sharing it with others?

I have never doubted the fact of my parents loving me, or each other, my friends loving their family members. I've never questioned my friends' marrying the guys they loved and the reciprocity of their feelings. We just knew it. But I can't remember any of them telling how they understood they were in love verbalizing it in three words: *I love you.* There were other nonverbal demonstrations of love with sending flowers and gifts involved, going to movies, or just walking in the streets and hanging out in parks, with hugs and occasional kissing throughout. While falling in love had all of its romantic attributes, it still retained a slightly forbidden flair when talking about it openly. We read about the great, breathtaking love stories in books, read poems, we watched movies, but in our every day lives, we were not used to expressing our love openly. Neither to our loved ones nor our friends. I can't remember telling any of my friends that I loved them.

The fact that we were friends already meant it. Sharing secrets, spending all the time together, chatting on the phone for hours, wanting to be together, and being with each other through all the good and bad, already encompassed love, as we understood it. There was no need to say it aloud. We hid those "I Love You"s under the covers in our bedrooms with a huge 'Private Space' sign hanging. Of course, we talked about sex or the lack of it, but even in very close friendships, discussing our sexual experiences was an inner circle thing, something you'd prefer to keep to yourself. While sex was considered private, love needed no proof; up until all of a sudden, the social media shifted it all, setting different rules of communication, and those super –techy phones invaded our lives. We went to customizable templates for sending handwritten notes or letters, from calling our friends or family members to sending text messages with emojis that we thought would show our emotions.

Social media became a universe filled with an outpour of love, visible and articulated. A virtual reality where friends compliment each other endlessly, where proud moms post about every step of their children, where children publicly thank their parents and express their gratitude for being brought into this world. We started celebrating our friendships online. We started dating online, traveling, shopping online, and posting excessively to our social media accounts. We got used that commenting with a heart emoji under a friend's post is enough, uncomplicated, and straightforward. Somewhere along the way, we decided it's time to show our feelings plain open to the outside world, and that's when I think we lost it. We transformed it from unsaid yet real to shouted on top of our lungs but fake. I often wonder what my grandparents would do if they had social media accounts. How frequently would they post, and what? Pictures from their youth? Motivational quotes? Would they post something like, "I'm so happy you were born my love" on their loved one's birthdays? Would they celebrate friendships and tag their friends? Would they participate in political discussions? Would they share recipes? Would they blog? Would they eagerly share updates from their personal lives? Post pictures from cafes and restaurants they've visited? To be honest, I doubt. I think they were from the era when privacy was essential, when our private world had boundaries...When *love* was often whispered, but true...

VII

September 2020

30

Confessions by the Sea

I t was alive, that early September sea. Calm, velvety, soothing, almost silky. I swam, trying to focus on a thin line of the sunset reflected on its surface. "Aren't you coming back?" My mom called me from afar, and suddenly, right then, I realized with all intensity that this moment of pure bliss of a warm, calm September evening may never return. We may, of course, come back to this tiny Georgian village by the seaside, where cows are freely marching on the shore. Stray dogs are bathing their furry bodies in the sea waves, where pine and eucalyptus trees accompany you as you walk to the beach, inhaling their unmistakable smell, but it will still be different. It hit me full force, how unprepared we are for the future, which, no matter how well we plan it, yet, is entirely unpredictable.

I don't know why the realization of life's finality came to me right that moment, not earlier or afterward in all its clarity, and what triggered that thought, but as I remember this small episode in the sea, I'm returning to it more and more often now.

It's not the fear of death I'm worried about; instead, it's a fear of the unknown, the fear of instability, the fear of losing your family members, friends, loved ones, the fear of being unable to protect them. The fear of not knowing how we will live next year and what's gonna happen considering the global pandemic. It seems we may need something more tangible than words and happy wishes. And, it's not just about the strange times we're now living in, there, swimming what seemed happily in the sea, it occurred to me that I've wasted too much time, I've postponed many things for the future, and very rarely lived genuinely enjoying the moment. Meanwhile, the clock is ticking....

About the Author

Nino Gugunishvili's writing biography includes a collection of short stories, " You Will Have a Black Labrador," and a women's fiction novel " Friday Evening, Eight O' Clock."

Also by Nino Gugunishvili

You Will Have a Black Labrador

Love, memories, family, enduring friendships, cooking, movies, dogs, travels, hairstyles, and saying Yes to many No's in a witty, yet often sentimental, journey of self-discovery... You Will Have a Black Labrador is a collection of semi-autobiographical essays forming a narrative about a modern Georgian woman. Her stories range from the search for a perfect romantic partner to exploring food as an integral part of the Georgian culture. Many of the vignettes center on childhood memories or weird family traditions, such as the way family members stay connected, no matter if they're deceased or alive. One essay reveals how making a simple omelette can change your life; and that No can be the most powerful word in any language. She shows us, too, that a haircut can be a tribute to the movies you love as well as a path to your freedom; and how owning a dog always brings unexpected experiences. In this poignantly humourous collection, reality mixes and interferes with an imaginative world in so many surprising ways.

Tasha is a dreamer in search of a new dream. She's bored with Pilates. She's never tried yoga. She doesn't even have a driver's license. She lives a pretty ordinary life as a freelance writer who battles the occasional flow of melancholy with the regular flow of martinis. Nestled into her couch, her television remote in one hand and a cold adult beverage in the other, shes found a favorite way to pass the hours on a Friday evening. It's comfortable and familiar, but it's not exactly an exciting way to live. With two of her closest friends, a bossy mother, an eighty-two-year-old grandmother, and Griffin, her fat yellow Labrador, at her side, she knows that there has to be something better out there. But where? When she gets an unexpected offer to relocate to France to write a magazine column, she thinks her circumstances are improving. But life in a new country isn't all peches et la creme. Now far away from her comfort zone, Tasha must find the inner strength to start a new career and navigate the bizarre and unknown world of professional jealousy, intrigue, and conflicting personalities in a very foreign land. It's enough to make a girl yearn for those quiet nights on the couch.

Printed in Great Britain
by Amazon